THE OFFICIAL
TOTTENHAM HOTSPUR
ANNUAL 2019

TOTTENHAM
HOTSPUR

Written by Andy Greeves
Designed by Chris Dalrymple

A Grange Publication

©2018. Published by Grange Communications Ltd., Edinburgh, under licence from Tottenham Hotspur Ltd. Printed in the EU.

Photography © PA Image

ISBN 978-1-912595-20-4

D1418220

CONTENTS

INTRODUCTION

Dear Supporters,

Welcome to the 2019 Official Tottenham Hotspur Annual.

It's a hugely exciting and proud time to be a Spurs supporter. Under the management of Mauricio Pochettino, the Club achieved qualification for the UEFA Champions League for the third consecutive year in 2018 while no less than 12 of our players turned out at that summer's FIFA World Cup in Russia. Domestically, Jan Vertonghen, Christian Eriksen and Harry Kane were all named in the PFA Premier League Team of the Year, while Kane bagged two Premier League Player of the Month awards during the campaign as we finished third in the league.

In this Annual, we'll look back on another memorable campaign in 2017/18, which included victories over the likes of Arsenal, Chelsea, Liverpool, Manchester United and European champions Real Madrid. All your favourite players are profiled, while we learn more about the Club's history and relive some of our best goals from last season. There are also quizzes, games and posters and plenty more besides.

Enjoy your new Annual and COME ON YOU SPURS!

#COYS

Andy Greeves

TOP TEN PREMIER LEAGUE GOALS OF THE SEASON

A look back at some of Tottenham Hotspur's best Premier League goals in 2017/18.

10 – Harry Kane v Southampton (home)

Harry completed his hat-trick in a comfortable 5-2 victory over Southampton in real style. Getting on the end of a Dele Alli through-ball, the England marksman lifted his shot over the head of the on-rushing goalkeeper Fraser Forster with his left foot. The Boxing Day strike was Harry's 37th in the Premier League in 2017, which saw him surpass Alan Shearer's 1995 record for the most goals in the division in a calendar year.

9 – Dele Alli v Chelsea (away)

Eric Dier's raking pass during our 3-1 win at Chelsea in April 2018 was controlled with one touch from Dele Alli. As the England man bore down on Willy Caballero, his second contact with the ball saw him lift it over the Blues keeper to put us 2-1 up.

8 – Harry Kane v Arsenal (home)

Harry has had a uncanny knack of scoring goals in the north London derby during his career. His powerful header from a Ben Davies cross against the Gunners in February 2018 gave us all three points in a 1-0 win.

7 – Christian Eriksen v Manchester United (home)

Timed at just eleven seconds, Christian Eriksen scored the fastest goal of the Premier League season in a 2-0 win over the Red Devils. Jan Vertonghen's long pass from his own half was headed on by Harry Kane into the United box. Dele Alli's flick was collected by the Dane, who made no mistake from close range.

6 – Ben Davies v Huddersfield Town (away)

After Harry Kane gave us an early lead at the John Smith's Stadium back in September 2017, Ben Davies doubled our advantage, finishing off a fine team move. Toby Alderweireld, Eric Dier, Kieran Trippier, Dele Alli, Christian Eriksen and Kane were all involved in a neat, one-touch passing exchange before the Welshman slotted past Jonas Lossl in the Terriers goal.

5 – Harry Kane v Huddersfield Town (away)

While Davies' goal at Huddersfield was all about great team play, Kane's second goal in the 4-0 win was a moment of individual brilliance. Collecting a Kieran Trippier throw-in with his back to goal, the England skipper held the ball up. He turned and evaded the challenge of a number of Town defenders before curling a fine, left-footed shot past Lossl from the edge of the Terriers' penalty area.

4 – Heung-Min Son v Crystal Palace (home)

In a tight London derby, Sonny got on to a misplaced clearance by Yohan Cabaye on the edge of the penalty area midway through the second-half. The South Korean took a touch to set himself, before firing a left-footed effort past Julian Speroni. Son's match-winner saw him become the highest goal scorer from Asia in Premier League history.

3 – Heung-Min Son v West Ham United (home)

Another long range piledriver from Sonny helped us secure a 1-1 draw with West Ham at the start of 2018. Collecting a pass from Erik Lamela, our number seven was offered a clear sight at goal from all of 30 yards. He had no hesitation, smashing the ball with his right boot beyond the despairing dive of Hammers stopper Adrian.

2 – Christian Eriksen v Chelsea (away)

In stoppage time at the end of the first half at Stamford Bridge in April 2018, Christian collected a ball from Ben Davies around 30 yards from the Chelsea goal. The Dane's long-range effort dipped, swerved and deceived Blues stopper Willy Caballero, sending us in level at the break during our famous 3-1 away win.

1 – Victor Wanyama v Liverpool (away)

When Reds goalkeeper Loris Karius punched away a dangerous looking Christian Eriksen cross, he must have thought he had averted the Spurs threat for the time being. After the Reds couldn't fully clear, the ball rolled into the path of Wanyama, and the Kenyan's first-time strike from all of 30 yards was hit with such venom that it nearly burst the net at Anfield's Kop end!

PREMIER LEAGUE SEASON REVIEW - 2017/2018

The 2017/2018 season saw Spurs finish in the Premier League's top three and secure UEFA Champions League football for a third campaign in a row. Playing 'home' matches at our temporary base of Wembley Stadium, Mauricio Pochettino's team impressed, winning 23 and drawing eight of their 38 league games and scoring 74 goals in the process. Star men Jan Vertonghen, Christian Eriksen and Harry Kane were all included in the PFA's Premier League Team of the Year on the back of their fine individual performances during the season.

AUGUST

Goals from Dele Alli and Ben Davies gave us the perfect start to the 2017/18 season, as we won 2-0 at Newcastle United on the opening weekend of the campaign. Our first Premier League match at Wembley Stadium saw us take on London rivals Chelsea. Despite a good performance from Spurs and a Michy Batshuayi own-goal, it was the Blues who ran out 2-1 winners. The following week, we drew 1-1 with Burnley at Wembley, with Dele on target once again.

SEPTEMBER

We were unbeaten in the Premier League during the month of September, with three wins and a draw. Two goals from Harry Kane and a further strike from Christian Eriksen gave us an impressive 3-0 victory at Everton, with Kane's first goal his 100th for the club. Our goalless draw with Swansea City at Wembley was followed by a brilliant 3-2 triumph over rivals West Ham United. Kane got two of our goals at the London Stadium, while Eriksen also scored. Kane's red-hot form continued with another brace in our 4-0 win at Huddersfield Town, while Davies and Moussa Sissoko found the back of the net in that game too.

OCTOBER

Eriksen's second-half goal saw us beat AFC Bournemouth 1-0 at Wembley Stadium in our first Premier League match of October. A week later, a crowd of 80,827 was treated to one of our best home performances of the season as we hammered Liverpool 4-1. Goals from Kane, Heung-Min Son and Dele had put us 3-1 up before the half-time whistle sounded. Kane scored again in the second-half to complete a memorable result. We ended the month with a narrow 1-0 defeat at Manchester United.

NOVEMBER

While November saw us get some fantastic results in the UEFA Champions League the month was less memorable in the Premier League. After beating Crystal Palace 1-0 at Wembley, thanks to a Son strike, we lost 2-0 to Arsenal at the Emirates Stadium in the first north London derby of the season. Kane scored in our two remaining fixtures of the month as we drew 1-1 at home to West Bromwich Albion and were defeated 2-1 at Leicester City

DECEMBER

December was our busiest month of the season, with no less than six Premier League matches scheduled. Son scored in the first of those fixtures as we drew 1-1 with Watford. Sonny also netted in our impressive 5-1 win over Stoke City at Wembley, that featured a brace from Kane, a Ryan Shawcross own-goal and a further strike from Eriksen. Four days later, we beat Brighton & Hove Albion 2-0, with Serge Aurier scoring his first goal for Spurs that night. Son was also on the scoresheet for the third league match in a row.

Eventual Premier League champions Manchester City beat us 4-1 at the Etihad Stadium during the month, with Eriksen's late goal proving to be nothing but a consolation. Kane got a hat-trick in our 3-0 victory at Burnley and our Boxing Day bonanza that saw us beat Southampton 5-2 at Wembley Stadium. Dele and Son were also on target against the Saints.

JANUARY

At the start of January Fernando Llorente scored against his old club Swansea City as we won 2-0 at the Liberty Stadium. Dele wrapped up the victory in South Wales with an 89th minute goal.

Son hit a stunning long-range goal in our 1-1 draw against West Ham United at Wembley Stadium two days later. Sonny netted again in our 4-0 thrashing of Everton, with Kane getting a brace and Eriksen also scoring against the Toffees.

Kane's strike in a 1-1 draw at home to Southampton came 10 days before one of our matches of the season – a 2-0 victory over Manchester United at Wembley Stadium at the end of the month. Eriksen's opener after just 11 seconds against the Red Devils was the quickest goal of the campaign and the third fastest in Premier League history. Phil Jones' own-goal saw us complete the victory against Jose Mourinho's team.

FEBRUARY

Our unbeaten start to 2018 continued throughout February, with a string of impressive results. Victor Wanyama's 'Goal of the Month' contender in our 2-2 draw with Liverpool came during an incredible match that saw Kane secure a point with a stoppage time penalty.

Six days later, Kane netted again in our 1-0 triumph over Arsenal at Wembley Stadium. Our north London derby victory was watched by a crowd of 83,222 – our biggest-ever attendance for a home league match. Kane's third goal of the month saw us win 1-0 at Crystal Palace.

MARCH

Son's brace in our 2-0 win at home to Huddersfield Town at the start of March continued our unbeaten run in the Premier League to 11 matches. The South Korean also scored twice as we secured a 4-1 victory at AFC Bournemouth, with further goals from Dele and Aurier.

APRIL

No Spurs supporter will ever forget our 3-1 win at Chelsea on 1 April, 2018 as it was our first victory at Stamford Bridge since 1990. Goals from Eriksen and a brace from Dele capped a magnificent performance from Mauricio Pochettino's men. Eriksen and Kane scored in our 2-1 win at Stoke City six days later as we cemented our position in the Premier League table's top four.

Our run of 14 league matches unbeaten finally fell at home to champions-elect Manchester City. Eriksen got our consolation in the 3-1 defeat watched by another 80,000-plus crowd at Wembley Stadium. Kane scored in our 1-1 draw at Brighton & Hove Albion while we ended the month with a 2-0 win over Watford thanks to strikes from Dele and Kane.

MAY

A disappointing 1-0 defeat at West Bromwich Albion at the start of May failed to halt our march to a third-placed finish in the Premier League. Kane's goal in our 1-0 home triumph over Newcastle United a few days later confirmed our top four place and UEFA Champions League qualification for a third successive season.

We ended the campaign with a crazy 5-4 win over Leicester City at Wembley. Kane and Erik Lamela both scored twice in the victory that also featured a Christian Fuchs own-goal.

NIGHTS TO REMEMBER!

Our 2017/2018 UEFA Champions League produced some memorable moments, as we topped Group H and progressed to the last 16 of the competition.

Group H

Matchday One
Spurs 3-1 Borussia Dortmund

Heung-Min Son's fourth-minute strike set us on the way to a fantastic 3-1 victory over German side Borussia Dortmund in our first UEFA champions League match of the season. Andriy Yarmolenko equalised moments later but goals from Harry Kane either side of half-time secured all three points for us at Wembley.

Matchday Two
APOEL 0-3 Spurs

Cypriot champions APOEL were no match for Mauricio Pochettino's team on Matchday Two, as a Kane hat-trick in Nicosia made it six points out of six for us at the top of Group H.

Matchday Three
Real Madrid 1-1 Spurs

A determined performance saw us gain a highly credible draw away to European champions Real Madrid on Matchday Three. We took the lead at the Santiago Bernabéu after 28 minutes when Serge Aurier's cross was put into the back of his own net by Real's Raphaël Varane. Cristiano Ronaldo scored a penalty to level for the Spanish team just before half-time while there were chances for both sides to win the game in the second period.

Matchday Four
Spurs 3-1 Real Madrid

On 1 November 2017, a crowd of 83,782 were present to see one of our finest performances in European competition. By the 65th minute of this encounter with the eventual tournament winners Real Madrid, we were 3-0 up thanks to a brace from Dele Alli and a Christian Eriksen finish. Ronaldo's late goal proved nothing more than a consolation for the Spanish giants, on a real 'Glory Glory Night' for Spurs at Wembley.

Matchday Five
Borussia Dortmund 1-2 Spurs

An impressive 2-1 away victory in Germany saw us secure top spot in Group H with a match still to play. Pierre-Emerick Aubameyang put the hosts ahead at half-time at the Westfalenstadion but second-half strikes from Kane and Son gave us our fourth Champions League win of the campaign.

Matchday Six
Spurs 3-0 APOEL

Our triumphant Group H campaign was rounded off with a comfortable 3-0 win over APOEL at Wembley, which featured goals from Fernando Llorente, Son and Georges-Kévin Nkoudou.

Round of 16

Round of 16, first leg
Juventus 2-2 Spurs

Two goals from Gonzalo Higuaín in the opening nine minutes gave Juventus early control of the Round of 16 match in Turin. A magnificent fightback saw us leave Italy with honours even though, as goals either side of half-time from Kane and Eriksen secured a 2-2 draw.

Round of 16, second leg
Spurs 1-2 Juventus

For the majority of our second leg meeting with Juventus at Wembley, we were the better side in terms of possession and chances – managing 23 shots to the Italians' eight. Son gave us a deserved lead on 39 minutes, in front of 84,010 spectators – our largest home crowd of the season. The visitors showed their experience in Europe's premier club competition by scoring twice in three second-half minutes through Higuaín and Paulo Dybala. A Kane header in the closing seconds beat Juve goalkeeper Gianluigi Buffon but unfortunately, the ball hit the post and bounced agonisingly along the goal line before being cleared.

FA CUP REVIEW

Third Round – Spurs 3-0 AFC Wimbledon

Three goals in eight second-half minutes gave us a comfortable 3-0 victory over AFC Wimbledon at Wembley in the third round. A brace from Harry Kane was followed with a fine, long range strike from One Hotspur Player of the Season, Jan Vertonghen.

Fourth Round – Newport County 1-1 Spurs

League Two club Newport County – who had beaten Championship side Leeds United in the previous round – took a shock first half lead against us at Rodney Parade through Pádraig Amond. Kane's leveller, with eight minutes of the match remaining, ensured an upset was avoided.

Replay – Spurs 2-0 Newport County

A Dan Butler own-goal and a further strike from Erik Lamela gave us a comfortable 2-0 victory over Newport County in the replay.

Fifth Round – Rochdale 2-2 Spurs

We met lower league opponents in the cup once again in round five as we travelled to Rochdale of League One. Goals from Lucas Moura and an 88th minute penalty from Kane – which cancelled out an earlier effort from Dale's Ian Henderson – looked to have secured our place in the quarter-finals. However, a stoppage time leveller from Steve Davies set-up our second replay in as many rounds.

Replay – Spurs 6-1 Rochdale

Amidst the snowfall at Wembley, we breezed past Rochdale in our fifth round replay. While the two teams went in level at the break – after Son's opener and Stephen Humphrys' equaliser for Dale – a second-half hat-trick from Llorente made sure of our victory. Another goal from Son and a stoppage time strike from Kyle Walker-Peters completed a 6-1 triumph.

Sixth Round – Swansea City 0-3 Spurs

We saw off our first Premier League opponents in the FA Cup en route to the semi-final of the competition as we beat Swansea City 3-0 at the Liberty Stadium. Christian Eriksen got two goals on the day either side of the half-time break, while Lamela was also on target in South Wales.

Semi-final – Manchester United 2-1 Spurs

Our bright start in our FA Cup semi-final was capped after 11 minutes when Dele Alli gave us the lead at Wembley. However the Red Devils grew in belief after Alexis Sánchez's equaliser before half-time and in the second-half, a strike from Ander Herrera saw United edge a hard-fought encounter to reach the final.

CARABAO CUP REVIEW

Third Round – Spurs 1-0 Barnsley

Argentinian defender Juan Foyth made his Spurs debut in our League Cup tie with Championship side Barnsley at Wembley. Dele Alli's 65th minute strike was enough to see off the Tykes as we progressed to a fourth round meeting with London rivals West Ham United.

Fourth Round – Spurs 2-3 West Ham United

We looked to be cruising into the fifth round of the League Cup when goals from Moussa Sissoko and Dele put us 2-0 up against the Hammers. We were made to pay for a number of missed opportunities to increase our lead as André Ayew's brace levelled for the East Londoners while Angelo Ogbonna got their winner.

THE KIDS ARE ALRIGHT!

Our young players took part in a variety of competitions during the 2017-18 season including…

Premier League 2

Our Under-23 side finished ninth in Premier League 2 with highlights including home and away victories over the likes of Arsenal and Manchester United, while we enjoyed a 2-1 win at Chelsea in the penultimate fixture of the campaign.

Under-18 Premier League

Our Under-18s ended their league season in impressive manner, beating rivals Arsenal 9-0 at Hotspur Way, as we claimed a fourth-place finish in the division.

UEFA Youth League

Four wins, a draw and just one defeat saw our Under-19 side top Group H of the UEFA Youth League, which contained Real Madrid, Borussia Dortmund and APOEL. Progress in the competition continued as our youngsters beat Monaco on penalties after the round of 16 clash finished in a 1-1 draw at Stevenage's Broadhall Way before elimination at the quarter final stage by Porto.

Checkatrade Trophy

In 2017-18, our development squad entered the Checkatrade Trophy, for the first time. Pitted against the first teams of Football League sides Luton Town, AFC Wimbledon and Barnet, we failed to make it out of Group F (Southern Section) of the competition despite some pleasing performances.

Premier League International Cup

Our Under-23 side took on Benfica, Villarreal and West Ham United in Group F of the Premier League International Cup. A 7-2 victory over the Hammers and a 3-3 draw with Benfica sadly wasn't enough to see Wayne Burnett's side progress to the quarter finals of the competition.

Under-18 Premier League Cup

We beat the likes of Leicester City, Aston Villa, Liverpool and Arsenal en route to the final of the newly-introduced Under-18 Premier League Cup. Chelsea's Under-18s claimed the silverware, with a 2-0 victory over us at the Blues' Cobham training base.

FA Youth Cup

A 5-0 victory over Preston North End and a 3-0 win at AFC Bournemouth saw our Under-18s progress to the fifth round of the FA Youth Cup. We were eliminated at that stage by Chelsea, who went on to claim the trophy for the fifth year in a row in 2018.

HE'S ONE OF OUR OWN!

With his commitment to be the very best, not to mention his goal scoring prowess, Harry Kane continues to raise the bar when it comes to his performance levels.

Harry Kane was the toast of a nation as he captained England to the semi-finals of the FIFA World Cup in the summer of 2018. The Walthamstow-born striker won the tournament's Golden Boot too with six goals in seven matches as the Three Lions finished fourth in the competition overall.

Harry's performances in Russia came on the back of another wonderful season for Spurs. His 41 strikes in 48 appearances for us in all competitions in 2017-18 made it his most prolific campaign in our colours yet, as he took his overall Spurs goals tally to 140 in 213 matches by the end of that season.

There were a number of significant landmarks during the season for Harry. In October 2017, he was the only Englishman to be included on the 30-player Ballon d'Or shortlist and was later named the tenth best player in the world overall. In January 2018, he became our top goal scorer of the Premier League era with his second goal in a brace against Everton seeing him surpass Teddy Sheringham's tally of 97. He was also named in the PFA Team of the Year for the fourth consecutive time at the end of 2017-18 season.

Kane has had quite a journey since originally joining our youth academy as an 11-year-old back in 2004. He put pen-to-paper on a scholarship on his 16th birthday in July 2009 and signed his first professional contract with us a year later. Loaned to Leyton Orient during the second-half of the 2010-11 season, the striker's league debut came as a substitute in the O's 1-1 draw at Rochdale on January 15, 2011. Loan moves to the likes of Millwall, Norwich City and Leicester City followed.

Born: 28 July 1993   Position: Forward

Height(m): 1.88   Weight(kg): 86

Previous Club(s): Leyton Orient (loan), Millwall (loan), Norwich City (loan), Leicester City (loan)

Squad Number: 10

Kane's first team debut in our colours came in a goalless draw with Heart of Midlothian in the UEFA Europa League on August 25, 2011. His first goal for us came in the same competition a few months later as we won 4-0 away at Shamrock Rovers.

Kane's Premier League debut came as a substitute in our 2-1 defeat at Newcastle United on the opening weekend of the 2012-13 season. He spent the majority of the campaign thereafter at Norwich and Leicester. His real 'breakthrough' season came in 2013-14 as he scored four goals in 19 appearances for us while he became a first team regular in 2014-15 with an impressive 31 strikes in 51 games. He was voted PFA Young Player of the Year at the end of the campaign and also took his place in the PFA Premier League Team of the Year for the first time.

Any suggestions of Kane being a 'one season wonder' were quickly rebuffed as the striker became a model of consistency with 28 goals in 50 club matches in 2015-16 and 35 strikes in 38 games in 2016-17. With supporters regarding him as 'one of our own', it was perhaps fitting that Harry scored our last-ever goal at White Hart Lane in our final match there against Manchester United in May 2017.

Harry also scored after just 79 seconds of his international debut, after being introduced as a substitute for the Three Lions against Lithuania in March 2015. He scored five times in seven 2018 FIFA World Cup qualifying appearances, as England topped their group with eight wins and two draws in their ten matches. By the end of the 2018 FIFA World Cup, he had netted 19 times in 30 internationals.

On top of having been named in the PFA Premier League Team of the Year for the last four successive seasons, Kane has also scooped the Premier League Player of the Month award on no less than six occasions at the time of writing – the most recent occasion being December 2017 – while he was the division's Golden Boot winner in both 2015-16 and 2016-17.

Signed, Sealed, Delivered

In June 2018, Harry put pen-to-paper on a new six-year contract with the Club that runs until 2024.

"I'm really excited, it's a proud day," said Kane on signing the new deal. "Obviously it's been a great few seasons and I'm looking forward to the future. It's been fantastic to consistently get in the Champions League so I'm really excited to have another go at that and with the Premier League and FA Cup, we'll look to go as far as we can. For us as a Club, it's just about keeping improving and we'll work hard to do that."

NICE ONE SONNY!

Born: 8 July 1992
Position: Forward
Height(m): 1.83
Weight(kg): 77
Previous Club(s):
Hamburg, Bayer
Leverkusen
Squad Number: 7

South Korean-ace Heung-Min Son continues to endear himself to teammates and supporters alike with his work rate, skill and goal-scoring ability.

Heung-Min Son's winning goal against Crystal Palace in November 2017 saw him become the top Asian scorer in Premier League history, surpassing compatriot Park Ji-Sung's total of 19 goals for Manchester United between 2005 and 2012. By the end of the campaign, Sonny had extended his own record, with 12 strikes in the division in 2017/18 taking his number of Premier League goals to 30 overall.

Having arrived from Bayer Leverkusen in the summer of 2015, the Chuncheon-born forward found the back of the net eight times in 40 matches in all competitions for us in his debut season. He followed that up with 21 strikes in 47 games in 2016/17 and 18 goals in 52 appearances in 2017/18.

Son got our 2017/18 UEFA Champions League campaign off to a real flyer, with a goal after just four minutes of our opening group game against Borussia Dortmund. We went on to win 3-1 at Wembley that evening, with the South Korean also netting in our away win in Dortmund and in a 3-0 home triumph against APOEL in Group H. He made it four goals in seven appearances in the competition overall, with a strike against Juventus at Wembley in the knockout phase.

Sonny's first goal in the Premier League during the 2017/18 campaign came in a 4-1 home victory over Liverpool in October 2017 prior to the aforementioned effort against Palace the following month. When he gave us the lead in our 4-0 win over Everton in January 2018, he became only the second player to score in five consecutive home Premier League matches for us since Jermain Defoe back in 2004. The South Korean's run saw him net against Stoke City, Brighton & Hove Albion, Southampton, West Ham United and the Toffees at Wembley. He also bagged a brace in our 6-1 victory over Rochdale in the FA Cup in 2018.

Of course, there's more to Sonny's game than 'just' goals. The South Korean international managed 13 assists in the Premier League in his first three seasons with us and his overall play saw him named AFC's International Footballer of the Year in 2015 and 2017. He was the recipient of the Premier League Player of the Month award in September 2016 and April 2017, meanwhile as well as the PFA Fans' Premier League Player of the Month award in January 2018.

THE REAL DEAL

One of the biggest talents in world football right now, Dele Alli is looking to continue his excellent form of recent seasons for both club and country.

Along with club mates Harry Kane, Danny Rose, Kieran Trippier and Eric Dier, Dele Alli was another Spurs player to appear for the Three Lions at the 2018 FIFA World Cup. The Milton Keynes-born attacking midfielder started four of England's seven matches at the tournament and also came on as a substitute for Ruben Loftus-Cheek in the Third Place Play-Off against Belgium. Earlier in the competition, his header sealed a 2-0 quarter-final victory over Sweden in Samara, confirming England's place in their first World Cup semi-final since 1990.

Dele's career began with his home town team MK Dons, for whom he scored 24 goals in 88 appearances during a permanent and loan spell with the club between 2012 and 2015. He signed for us in 2015, making his Spurs debut away to Manchester United on the opening day of the 2015-16 season. Two weeks later, he got his first goal in our colours in a 1-1 draw at Leicester City.

In his first three seasons with us, Dele scored 46 goals in 146 matches. Having represented England at Under-17, Under-18, Under-19 and Under-21 levels, our number 20 made his senior international debut as an 88th minute substitute for Ross Barkley in the Three Lions' 2-0 victory over Estonia at Wembley Stadium on October 9, 2015. Up to and including England's final match at the 2018 FIFA World Cup, Dele had won 30 senior caps, scoring three times.

In his debut season with us, Dele made 46 appearances and netted ten times. He scored the BBC Match of the Day 'Goal of the Season' that campaign, as his fine volley helped us to a 3-1 win against Crystal Palace in January 2016. Unsurprisingly, given his scintillating form, Dele was the winner of the 2015-16 PFA Young Player of the Year. He also scooped the award in 2016-17, during a season in which he netted 22 times in 50 appearances for us.

Amongst Dele's 14 goals in 50 appearances for us in 2017-18 was a brace in our 3-1 home victory over European champions Real Madrid in the UEFA Champions League. He also scored twice as we won 3-1 at Chelsea in April 2018 – our first triumph at Stamford Bridge since 1990.

Born: 11 April 1996
Position: Midfielder
Height(m): 1.88
Weight(kg): 80
Previous Club(s): MK Dons
Squad Number: 20

SUPER SPURS STATS 2017-18

Our third-placed Premier League finish guaranteed our third consecutive season in the UEFA Champions League.

Our points tally of 77 was our second-best return of the Premier League era, bettered only by the 86 points that took us to the division's runners-up spot in 2016/17.

We equalled our best-ever unbeaten run in the Premier League during the season, going 14 matches in the division without defeat. The run started with a 3-0 victory at Burnley in December 2017 before ending with a 3-1 defeat to champions Manchester City in April 2018. We managed 11 wins and three draws during the run – which betters our return of six wins and eight draws set during our other 14-match unbeaten stretch in the Premier League set between August and December 2015.

Harry Kane's brace in our 4-0 victory over Everton in January 2018 saw him equal and then break Teddy Sheringham's club record tally of 97 Premier League goals. By the end of the campaign, Kane had extended the record to 108 Premier League goals in our colours.

Pos	Team	Pld	W	D	L	GF	GA	GD	Pts
1	Manchester City	38	32	4	2	106	27	+79	100
2	Manchester United	38	25	6	7	68	28	+40	8
3	Tottenham Hotspur	38	23	7	8	74	36	+38	77
4	Liverpool	38	21	12	5	84	38	+46	75
5	Chelsea	38	21	7	10	62	38	+24	70
6	Arsenal	38	19	6	13	74	51	+23	63
7	Burnley	38	14	12	12	36	39	-3	54
8	Everton	38	13	10	15	44	58	-14	49
9	Leicester City	38	12	11	15	56	60	-4	47
10	Newcastle United	38	12	8	18	39	37	-8	44
11	Crystal Palace	38	11	11	16	45	55	-10	44
12	Bournemouth	38	11	11	16	45	61	-16	44
13	West Ham United	38	10	12	16	48	68	-20	42
14	Watford	38	11	8	19	44	64	-20	41
15	Brighton & Hove Albion	38	9	13	16	34	54	-20	40
16	Huddersfield Town	38	9	10	19	28	58	-30	37
17	Southampton	38	7	15	16	37	56	-19	36
18	Swansea City (R)	38	8	9	21	28	56	-28	33
19	Stoke City (R)	38	7	12	19	35	68	-33	33
20	West Bromwich Albion (R)	38	6	13	19	31	56	-25	31

We kept a club-record 16 Premier League clean sheets during the season – eclipsing the 15 stop-outs we managed in 2016/17.

Goalkeeper Hugo Lloris surpassed Ian Walker's club record for Premier League clean sheets during the season. The France number one's fourth stop-out of the campaign – in our 4-0 victory over Huddersfield Town in September 2017 – took him to 63 clean sheets in the league and beyond Walker's tally set in the division for us between 1992/93 and 2001. Lloris had extended the record to 74 Premier League clean sheets by the end of the season.

MAURICIO POCHETTINO

Mauricio Pochettino has overseen more matches than any other Spurs manager during the Premier League era, with our 5-4 victory over Leicester City on the final day of the 2017/18 season marking his 218th game in charge of the Club.

An Eric Dier goal gave us a 1-0 victory at West Ham United in Mauricio's first match as Spurs boss back in August 2014. In his debut season with the Club, we achieved a fifth-place finish in the Premier League, while we also reached the League Cup Final. Progress continued in 2015-16, as we came third in the Premier League – our best league finish since 1990 – and in 2016-17 we went one better by finishing as runners-up to champions Chelsea.

The 2017-18 season saw us secure memorable victories over the likes of Arsenal, Chelsea, Liverpool and Manchester United in the Premier League as we came third in the division and secured our place in the UEFA Champions League for a third consecutive season. No Spurs fan will ever forget our Champions League wins against teams such as Borussia Dortmund and European champions Real Madrid during the campaign while Mauricio also guided us to our second successive FA Cup semi-final in 2018.

At the end of the 2017/18 season, we were delighted to announce that Mauricio, along with his coaching staff

Jesús Pérez, Miguel D'Agostino and Toni Jiménez, had signed new five-year contracts with the Club, which run until 2023. At the time, the Argentine commented;

"I am honoured to have signed a new long-term contract as we approach one of the most significant periods in the Club's history and be the manager that will lead this team into our new world-class stadium.

"This is just one of the factors that makes this one of the most exciting jobs in world football and we are already making plans to ensure we continue to build on the great work that everyone has contributed to over the past four years.

"(Club Chairman) Daniel (Levy) and I have spoken at length about our aspirations for this football club. We both share the same philosophies to achieve long-term, sustainable success."

A win percentage of 55.5% at the end of the 2017/18 season makes Mauricio the second most successful manager in Spurs history after Frank Brettell in terms of his ratio of victories to draws and defeats. Widely recognised as one of the best managers in world football, the ex-Espanyol player has been named Premier League Manager of the Month on three occasions during his time with us up to and including the 2017/18 season.

Mauricio's Spurs Record

(All competitive, first-team matches up to and including the 2017-18 season)

Matches
Played: **218** Won: **121**
Drawn: **50** Lost: **47**
Win percentage: **55.5%**

MEET MAURICIO'S COACHING STAFF

Jesús Pérez
Assistant Manager

Jesús has previously worked with Mauricio as a Fitness Coach at Spanish club Espanyol, while he served as his Assistant Manager at Premier League side Southampton. The UEFA Pro Licence holder has almost two decades' experience of coaching, having also held posts with the likes of Al Ittihad, Almeria, Rayo Vallecano, Pontevedra, Real Murcia, Castellon and Tarragona.

Miguel D'Agostino
First Team Coach

Miguel is a former team-mate of 'Poch', with the pair having lined up in defence together for Argentine side Newell's Old Boys in the early 1990s. After stepping down from his role as Chief Scout at French side Brest, Miguel became part of Mauricio's coaching team at Espanyol. The Paraná-born coach followed him again to Southampton in 2013 and penned a contract with Spurs a year later.

Toni Jiménez
Goalkeeping Coach

Toni is a former Spanish international goalkeeper, who played over 350 league matches for the likes of Real Vallecano, Atletico Madrid and Elche during his career. It was at Espanyol where the La Garriga-born stopper met Mauricio. Five years after retiring from playing, Toni returned to the club as Goalkeeping Coach under Mauricio's management and since held the same role under him at Southampton and Spurs.

PLAYER PROFILES

Hugo Lloris

2018 was quite a year for Hugo, who captained France to World Cup glory in Russia. The goalkeeper also broke Ian Walker's club record of 62 Premier League clean sheets during the 2017/18 season - extending his tally to 74 stop-outs in the division by the end of the campaign. The France number one - who began his career with Nice - has made over 250 Spurs appearances since joining us from Lyon in 2013. He is captain of both country and club.

Michel Vorm

Michel has regularly featured in our cup matches since signing from Swansea City in the summer of 2014. The Dutch international, who signed a one-year extension to his Spurs contract during the summer of 2018, made 11 appearances for us during the 2017/18 season, starting all seven of our FA Cup ties.

Paulo Gazzaniga

Having previously played for Mauricio Pochettino at Southampton, Paulo was re-united with his former manager when he signed for us in August 2017. The Argentine stopper made an impressive Spurs debut, pulling off a series of good saves and keeping a clean sheet in our 1-0 Premier League victory over Crystal Palace in November 2017.

Kieran Trippier

Kieran has been in impressive form since joining Spurs from Burnley in 2015 and in addition to his defensive qualities, he offers a real threat going forward. In his first three seasons as a Spurs player, he made 19 assists in all competitions as well as scoring his first goal for us against Watford in his debut campaign. He was one of our five players included in the England squad for the 2018 FIFA World Cup.

Danny Rose

Danny is our longest serving first-team player, having arrived from Leeds United back in 2007. The Doncaster-born full-back scored a memorable goal on his Premier League debut for us against Arsenal in 2010 and has since featured in over 160 matches for us in all competitions. The pacey defender was another of our players named in Gareth Southgate's England squad for the 2018 FIFA World Cup.

Toby Alderweireld

A calming influence in our backline, Toby was sadly restricted to just 21 club appearances during the 2017/18 season due to injury. The former Ajax, Atletico Madrid and Southampton centre-back, who can also play as a full-back, was named One Hotspur Player of the Season and was also included in the PFA Premier League Team of the Year in his debut campaign back in 2015/16.

Jan Vertonghen

'Super Jan' was our One Hotspur Player of the Season in 2017/18, during a campaign in which he formed an impressive central defensive pairing with new arrival Davinson Sánchez. The former Ajax star is the most capped Belgian player ever with over 100 caps and represented his country at his second FIFA World Cup in 2018. He has featured in over 200 matches for us and twice been named in the PFA Premier League Team of the Year since joining us back in 2012.

Davinson Sánchez

Having signed from Ajax in August 2017, Davinson was quick to settle in at Spurs, making 41 appearances for us in all competitions in his debut season. The Colombian international started all eight of our UEFA Champions League matches during the campaign, putting in memorable individual displays against the likes of Borussia Dortmund and Real Madrid.

Serge Aurier

On the back of winning two Ligue 1 titles with Paris Saint-Germain, Ivory Coast international Serge signed for us in August 2017. The energetic right-back featured in 24 matches in his debut season for Spurs in which he netted in victories at home to Brighton & Hove Albion and away to AFC Bournemouth.

Ben Davies

In the absence of Danny Rose for much of the 2017/18 season, Ben pretty much made the Spurs left-back role his own, making 37 appearances in all competitions during the campaign and scoring twice. The Welsh international - who was part of the Dragons side that got to the semi-finals of UEFA Euro 2016 - has played over 100 games for us since signing from Swansea City in 2014.

Kyle Walker-Peters

Kyle rose through the ranks at Spurs to make his first-team debut for us away at Newcastle United on the opening weekend of the 2017/18 season. The talented full-back made nine appearances during the campaign, with his first goal in our colours coming against Rochdale in the FA Cup.

Juan Foyth

Juan established himself as a bright defensive talent with Argentinian Primera Division club Estudiantes prior to Mauricio Pochettino swooping to sign him in the summer of 2017. The centre-back made his first appearance for us against Barnsley in the League Cup in September 2017 and featured in eight matches overall during his debut campaign.

Cameron Carter-Vickers

Since playing four matches for us during the 2016/17 season, Cameron has been loaned to Sheffield United and Ipswich Town in order to build on his first-team experiences. Although he was born in England, the 6ft 1in defender represents the United States at international level.

Victor Wanyama

After signing for us from Southampton back in 2016, Victor quickly established himself as a midfield lynchpin at the Club. Best-known for his tough tackling and energetic displays, the Kenyan has also popped up with a number of important goals for us. His strike in our 2-2 draw at Liverpool in February 2018 was voted as the Premier League's Goal of the Month and our One Hotspur Goal of the Season.

Eric Dier

Able to play in a variety of positions, Eric has established himself as a regular for both club and country since joining us from Sporting Lisbon back in 2015. By the end of the 2017/18 season, the Cheltenham-born player was closing in on 200 appearances in our colours while he was named in England's squad for the 2018 FIFA World Cup.

Moussa Sissoko

Moussa arrived at Spurs from Newcastle United on transfer deadline day back in August 2016 and has since established himself as an important member of Mauricio Pochettino's squad. The energetic midfielder has won over 50 caps for France and made four starts at UEFA Euro 2016 as Les Bleus finished as tournament runners-up.

Mousa Dembélé

Mousa has been a model of consistency since signing from Fulham in August 2012, playing in 35-plus matches for us in each of his opening six seasons as a Spurs player. The Belgian international, who has appeared at two World Cups to date, is renowned for his strength and ability to pass opposition players at will.

Erik Lamela

Erik put his injury disappointments of recent years behind him to feature in 33 matches for us during the 2017/18 season, netting four times in the process. Having signed for us from Roma in 2013, the Argentine international has featured in over 150 matches for us to date. He wrote his name into Spurs folklore with his 'Rabona' wonder-goal against Asteras Tripolis in the UEFA Europa League back in October 2014.

Dele Alli

Dele's excellent form continued during the 2017/18 season, with the attacking midfielder scoring 14 goals in 50 appearances for us. Amongst his many highlights during the campaign was a brace in our 3-1 home victory over European champions Real Madrid in the UEFA Europa League while he also scored twice as we won 3-1 at Chelsea in April 2018. The two-time PFA Young Player of the Year was rewarded for his performances with a place in England's squad for the 2018 FIFA World Cup.

Christian Eriksen

Christian was one of three Spurs players to be named in the PFA Premier League Team of the Year in 2017/18 in recognition of a fine season that saw him net 14 times in 46 appearances for us. The Danish international also scooped the One Hotspur Junior Members' Player of the Season while his long-range effort against Chelsea in April 2018 was voted as the Premier League's Goal of the Month.

Lucas Moura

Arriving from Paris Saint-Germain in January 2018, Brazilian winger Lucas made his debut away to Juventus in the UEFA Champions League the following month. His first start and goal for the Club both came in our 2-2 draw at Rochdale in the FA Cup as he featured in 11 matches for us in total in the second-half of the 2017/18 season.

Harry Winks

A life-long Spurs fan, Harry got to fulfil a boyhood dream when he made his first team debut for us in a UEFA Europa League match in November 2014. The talented midfielder has since featured in over 60 matches for us and won his first cap for England away to Lithuania in October 2017.

Georges-Kévin Nkoudou

Georges-Kévin has largely been restricted to substitute appearances since his arrival from Marseille back in 2016. The winger spent a period on loan with Burnley in 2018 in a bid to get more Premier League experience, but scored his first Spurs goal in our Champions League home win against APOEL.

Josh Onomah

Josh is back at Spurs having spent the 2017/18 campaign on loan at Aston Villa, where he scored four goals in 33 appearances. The Enfield-born winger made his debut for us against Burnley in the FA Cup in 2015, with his first goal in our colours coming against Gillingham in the League Cup a year later. He was part of the England team that won the FIFA U-20 World Cup in 2017.

Heung-Min Son

Sonny is a real fans' favourite who can be relied upon to score important goals. The South Korean netted 47 times in 139 matches in his first three seasons with Spurs having arrived from German side Bayer Leverkusen in 2015. He has picked up a number of awards during his time in the Premier League, including the division's Player of the Month in September 2016 and April 2017. He also topped our social media vote for Goal of the Season in 2017/18 with a fine, long-range effort against Crystal Palace on November 2017.

Harry Kane

Harry helped fire England to the semi-finals of the 2018 FIFA World Cup with his six goals in six matches also seeing him collect the tournament's Golden Boot. Prior to travelling to Russia, the striker delighted Spurs supporters worldwide by putting pen to paper on a new contract in June 2018 that commits him to the Club until 2024. This came on the back of another excellent domestic season in 2017/18, that saw him become our top goal scorer of the Premier League era - surpassing Teddy Sheringham's tally of 97 strikes in a match against Everton in January 2018. He was also named in the PFA Premier League Team of the Year for a fourth consecutive time.

Fernando Llorente

A transfer deadline day signing from Swansea City back in August 2017, Fernando marked his first season at Spurs with five goals in 31 appearances. This included a hat-trick in our 6-1 defeat of Rochdale in the FA Cup while he netted on his first Premier League start for us away to his former club Swansea City in January 2018.

Vincent Janssen

Vincent spent the majority of the 2017/18 season on loan with Turkish club Fenerbahçe on the back of his debut campaign for Spurs in 2016/17 that saw him score six times in 35 matches. The Dutch international was awarded the Johan Cruyff Trophy in 2016, recognising him as the Netherlands' 'Talent of the Year'.

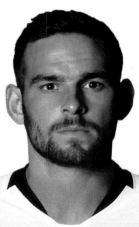

CAPTAIN MARVEL

Captain for club and country, World Cup winner Hugo Lloris is now in his seventh season with Spurs.

On July 15, 2018, Hugo Lloris became the first-ever Spurs player to captain his country to World Cup glory. France's 4-2 victory over Croatia in the final of Russia 2018 saw our long-serving goalkeeper lift the trophy at Moscow's Luzhniki Stadium.

"A lot of things happened in my mind and what a feeling to lift the trophy in front of your father, in front of your grandmother, in front of your daughters, in front of your wife, in front of my sister," reflected Hugo, on becoming the 21st World Cup-winning captain. "It is a big achievement but in football, you don't really have the time to enjoy it!"

Born in Nice on Boxing Day 1986, Hugo joined his local team OGC Nice's academy in 1997 at the age of ten. He rose through the ranks at the Côte d'Azur club, making his debut for Nice 'B' in 2005. His first-team debut followed later that year as he kept a clean sheet in a 2-0 Coupe de La Ligue victory over Châteauroux. The goalkeeper maintained his place in the starting line-up for Les Aiglons' other matches in the competition during the 2005/06 season, as they reached the final.

Hugo departed for Olympique Lyonnais in the summer of 2008 after 77 first-team appearances for Nice. The 6ft 2in stopper played in the UEFA Champions League for the first time in his debut season at Lyon, starting in all eight of the club's continental fixtures in 2008/09. He also won his first senior cap for France in a goalless draw with Uruguay during the campaign.

Nearly ten years on, Hugo's World Cup Final appearance in July 2018 was his 104th appearance for Les Bleus!

After 195 matches for Lyon, Hugo signed for Spurs in August 2012, with his debut coming in a UEFA Europa League match against Lazio the following month, while his first Premier League appearance was against Aston Villa on October 7, 2012. The goalkeeper's excellent form in his first three seasons with us saw him rewarded with the club captaincy at the start of the 2015/16 campaign.

Hugo has continued to excel in our colours, breaking Ian Walker's club record of 62 Premier League clean sheets during the 2017/18 season and extending that tally to 74 shut-outs in the division by the end of the campaign. On April 18, 2018, the French keeper made his 250th appearance for us in a 1-1 draw with Brighton & Hove Albion. In doing so, he became just the 61st Spurs player to achieve this milestone.

Born: 26 December 1986
Position: Goalkeeper
Height(m): 1.88
Weight(kg): 78
Previous Club(s): OGC Nice, Olympique Lyonnais
Squad Number: 1

WORDSEARCH

Can you find the names of EIGHT current and former Spurs players that have captained the Club?

```
L Y L K W L T K L C R X
N T H W L P N T W R E T
Q J C O K F G N R K W N
L F R K Z E L X N N O E
D I Q I L N A T J M L H
S K M N C N T N J Z F G
D G D G K U C X E H H N
L B P Q B L F M V R C O
V H Z B T N B R R Y N T
X P A L E N A K V T A R
B M L G N T M M N Y L E
P E R R Y M A N Z F B V
```

BLANCHFLOWER   KING

MABBUTT   LLORIS

PERRYMAN   KANE

KEANE   VERTONGHEN

Answers on page 61

NUMBERS GAME

Add the squad numbers to the back of these Spurs players' shirts...

DELE

VERTONGHEN

LLORIS

KANE

ERIKSEN

Complete the score lines from these famous Spurs victories...

1901 FA CUP FINAL	
SPURS	
SHEFFIELD UNITED	

1963 EUROPEAN CUP WINNERS' CUP FINAL	
SPURS	
ATLETICO MADRID	

PREMIER LEAGUE – OCT 2017	
SPURS	
LIVERPOOL	

1991 FA CUP SEMI-FINAL	
SPURS	
ARSENAL	

UEFA CHAMPIONS LEAGUE – NOV 2017	
SPURS	
REAL MADRID	

Answers on page 61

WORLD IN MOTION!

There were no less than 12 Spurs players in action in Russia, as the 2018 FIFA World Cup proved to be one of the most entertaining tournaments ever.

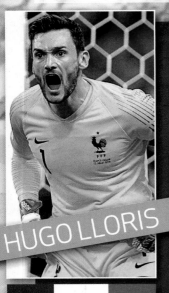

HUGO LLORIS

Hugo Lloris became the first Spurs player to captain a nation to World Cup glory, when he lifted the trophy after France's 4-2 victory over Croatia in the final of the tournament in Moscow on July 15, 2018. The goalkeeper started six of his country's seven fixtures in Russia, keeping three clean sheets along the way. England captain Harry Kane meanwhile won the competition's Golden Boot with six goals in seven appearances.

Lloris went head-to-head with Spurs teammate Christian Eriksen in Group C of the competition when France and Denmark were paired together. Both players started their opening fixtures as France beat Australia 2-1 and Denmark won 1-0 against Peru. Eriksen was then on target in the Denmark's 1-1 draw with Australia while the French captain kept a clean sheet as his side gained a 1-0 triumph over Peru. With qualification to the next round already secured, Lloris sat out France's final group game against Denmark but Eriksen started in the goalless draw.

Another Spurs match-up occurred in Group G, with England – represented by Dele Alli, Eric Dier, Danny Rose and Kieran Trippier as well as Harry – paired with Belgium, who included

Toby Alderweireld, Mousa Dembélé and Jan Vertonghen in their 23-man squad.

The Red Devils shaded the head-to-head meeting between the two nations in the final group fixture, with an Adnan Januzai goal giving them a 1-0 victory. Dier and Rose started the Kaliningrad match for England while Dembélé took to the field for Belgium. Both nations had already secured their place in the knockout phase prior that fixture with victories over Panama and Tunisia. Alderweireld and Vertonghen played the full 90 minutes for Belgium against those opponents while Kane and Trippier did likewise for England. Dembélé came on as a substitute in the Red Devils' 3-0 win over Panama.

HARRY KANE

Kane took an early lead in the race for the Golden Boot in his opening two matches at the tournament, scoring a brace in England's 2-1 win over Tunisia – a game in which Dele started and Dier came on as a substitute - and a hat-trick as the Three Lions thrashed Panama 6-1, which featured a substitute appearance from Rose.

Elsewhere, Heung-Min Son started all three of South Korea's Group F matches at the tournament, scoring a fine goal from outside of the box in a 2-1 defeat to Mexico. He was also on target in the Korean's 2-0 victory over Germany, which saw the four-time world champions eliminated from the competition. South Korea also failed to make it to the knock-out phase.

England went on to beat Davinson Sánchez's Colombia on penalties in the round of 16, with Kane on target once again in the match that finished in a 1-1 draw after extra-time. Kane, Trippier and Dier – along with Manchester United's Marcus Rashford – all scored as the Three Lions won 4-3 in the shootout. That match was the fourth and final fixture for Sánchez at the tournament. The central defender started all three Group H games for 'Los Cafeteros', who topped the table with victories over Poland and Senegal prior defeat to England in the last 16.

Elsewhere in the round of 16, Lloris was in goal for France for their incredible 4-3 victory over Argentina. Eriksen suffered the heartbreak of having a spot-kick saved in Denmark's 4-3 penalty shootout defeat to Croatia which followed a 1-1 draw between the two after extra-time. Vertonghen scored for Belgium in a thrilling match against Japan that saw the Red Devils come from 2-0 down to win 3-2.

HEUNG-MIN SON

JAN VERTONGHEN

Lloris' France continued their excellent form with a 2-0 triumph over Uruguay in the quarter-finals. Alderweireld and Vertonghen both started for Belgium in their impressive 2-1 win over Brazil at the same stage of the competition while Dele scored the second of England's goals in their 2-0 success over Sweden. Dele, Kane and Trippier started the match in Samara which also saw Dier come on as a late substitute.

A goal from Samuel Umtiti enabled France to see off Belgium in a Saint Petersburg semi-final that saw Lloris, Alderweireld, Dembélé and Vertonghen start for their respective nations. A wonderful Trippier free-kick put England ahead in their last four clash with Croatia. All five Spurs players in the Three Lions' squad were on the pitch at the Luzhniki Stadium in Moscow at one stage as substitutes Rose and Dier joined starters Dele, Kane and Trippier as Gareth Southgate's men went down to a 2-1 defeat after extra-time.

The day before an entertaining World Cup Final between France and Croatia, Belgium secured third place by beating England 2-0 in Saint Petersburg. Alderweireld and Vertonghen both started their sixth games for the Red Devils at the tournament while they were joined on the pitch by substitute Dembélé in the second-half. Dier, Kane, Rose and Trippier lined up for the Three Lions, while Dele was introduced late on.

ENGLAND TEAM

TOTTENHAM HOTSPUR
PLAYER DEVELOPMENT PROGRAMMES

COURSES FOR BOTH PLAYER DEVELOPMENT
AND COACH EDUCATION ARE AVAILABLE THROUGHOUT
EUROPE, ASIA AND AMERICA

Our scouting network is in operation across these programmes

tottenhamhotspur.com/holiday-courses

INTRODUCING CHIRPY AND LILY

Whenever Spurs are in action at the Tottenham Hotspur Stadium, you can be sure to see mascots Chirpy and Lily cheering on their favourite team...

On home matchdays, the pair meet fans and pose for selfies as the pre-match atmosphere builds. Around 30 minutes before kick-off, they lead a lucky group of our younger supporters (aged 5-15) – each waving a Spurs flag - around the perimeter of the pitch for Chirpy and Lily's Parade. The parade gets a huge cheer from each corner of the stadium, as the countdown to the start of the game continues.

It's not only on home matchdays that our feathery duo can be seen out and about. Keep your eyes eyes peeled for news of Chirpy and Lily's appearances in the local community as well as at charity initiatives and special events.

WE'RE THE FAMOUS TOTTENHAM HOTSPUR!

Amongst our vast legion of supporters are a number of well-known personalities who hold a special place in their hearts for Tottenham Hotspur.

Lord Alan Sugar

When he's not hiring and firing contestants on the BBC TV series The Apprentice, businessman Lord Sugar loves watching Spurs play. The Hackney-born entrepreneur also served as our Club chairman between 1991 and 2001.

Finn Balor

Wrestler Finn Balor started supporting Spurs as a child having been encouraged to do so by his brother Colin. The WWE superstar, who was born in the Republic of Ireland and now resides in the United States, has attended a number of our matches and also visited Hotspur Way.

Adele

For Tottenham-born singer Adele, it's a case of 'Hometown Glory' when it comes to her footballing loyalties. The multi-Brit Award winner was once pictured on-stage with a Spurs flag at one of her sell-out concerts, while she attended our FA Cup semi-final against Chelsea back in 2012.

Kenneth Branagh

Kenneth Branagh narrated an emotional video that was played after our final match at White Hart Lane in May 2017. The Belfast-born actor – who was inspired to support Spurs by our former double-winning captain and fellow Irishman Danny Blanchflower – has directed in a host of blockbuster films including Thor, Disney's Cinderella and the dramatic adaptation of Agatha Christie's Murder on the Orient Express.

Antony Costa

Antony Costa – best known as a member of the boyband Blue – has a blue and white family bloodline, with his mum and dad both having held Spurs season tickets. Antony attended his first match when he was just four.

Rupert Grint

Best known for his role as Ron Weasley in the Harry Potter films, actor Rupert Grint has attended numerous Spurs matches over the years, including our League Cup Final success at Wembley in 2008. It was Rupert's great granddad who introduced him to the Club.

Jude Law

Such is actor Jude Law's passion for Spurs, it is rumoured the scooter he rides in the film Alfie was painted blue and white especially as a tribute to his favourite football team!

Cher Lloyd

Singer Cher Lloyd is a keen Spurs follower, as is fellow former X Factor contestant Matt Cardle.

Candice Brown

Londoner Candice Brown, who won the seventh series of The Great British Bake Off back in 2016, is a life-long Spurs supporter.

Jessie J

Singer Jessie J sported a Spurs scarf and hoodie on a trip to White Hart Lane back in 2013, as she cheered us on in a match against Everton.

Steve Nash

NBA legend Steve Nash is a life-long Spurs supporter, with his father having been born in Tottenham. Nash's passion for football extends into his business interests, with the two-time NBA Most Valuable Player a part-owner of MLS side Vancouver Whitecaps FC and Spanish club RCD Mallorca.

Sam Warburton

As a youngster, Wales and British Lions rugby international and Spurs supporter Sam Warburton attended the same Cardiff school as our former forward Gareth Bale. Sam, who got to a number of our matches at Wembley last season, says he would like to become a Spurs season ticket holder when he retires from playing.

Emma Bunton

Radio presenter and former Spice Girl Emma Bunton has carried on a family tradition by supporting Tottenham Hotspur.

Adam Smith

Viewers of Sky Sports' Soccer AM will be familiar with Adam Smith - aka 'Smithy' or 'Frankie Fryer' - and his support for Spurs.

Michael McIntyre

Comedian and Big Show host Michael McIntyre can regularly be seen at Spurs matches cheering on his favourite team.

Devlin

Rapper Devlin came along to his first Spurs match against Leeds United when he was just six years old.

Sir Trevor McDonald

News-reading royalty Sir Trevor McDonald is a long-time Spurs fan who attended our north London derby victory against Arsenal last season.

Laura Kenny

Four-time Olympic gold medallist Laura Kenny was born into a family of Spurs supporters… with the one exception being her sister Emma, who follows Arsenal! The cyclist attended her first match against Blackburn Rovers when she was 12 years of age.

SPURS HISTORY IN TEN GREAT MOMENTS

Formed under a lamppost on Tottenham High Road back in September 1882, Tottenham Hotspur has risen from humble origins to become one of the most famous football clubs in the world. There have been countless highlights along the way, including these ten great moments…

1 – Cup Glory

In 1901, while playing in the old Southern League at the time, we became the first and only non-league club in the history of the FA Cup to win the competition. After drawing 2-2 with Sheffield United in the final, we beat the Blades 3-1 in the replay to lift the famous trophy for the first time.

2 – League Debutants

In 1908, we became members of the Football League. We finished as runners-up in the old Second Division in our debut league season in 1908/09 which saw us promoted to the top flight at the first time of asking!

3 – Title Success

In 1951, we became champions of England for the first time, as we finished four points clear of Manchester United at the top of the old First Division table. Arthur Rowe's team included England's future World Cup-winning boss Sir Alf Ramsey while Bill Nicholson was another regular in the starting line-up. 'Bill Nic', as he is affectionately known, became our manager in 1958 and guided us to no less than eight major trophy successes during his 16-year spell in charge of the club.

4 – Double Winners

In 1961, Nicholson's 'Super Spurs' team became the first club of the 20th century to win both the Football League title and the FA Cup in the same season. After winning 31 and drawing four of our 42 league matches that campaign, we beat Leicester City 2-0 in the FA Cup Final at Wembley to complete the 'Double'. Bill Nic's side won the FA Cup once again in 1962.

5 – Euro Stars

In 1963 - a year on from reaching the semi-final of the European Cup (now UEFA Champions League) - we became the first British club to win a major European competition. Jimmy Greaves, our all-time top goal scorer, netted twice in our 5-1 victory over Atletico Madrid in the European Cup Winners' Cup Final in Rotterdam to help claim the trophy. We won the FA Cup again in 1967, the League Cup in 1971 and 1973 as well as the UEFA Cup in 1972 under Nicholson's management.

6 – In Safe Hands

In 1984, two great saves from rookie goalkeeper Tony Parks saw us beat Belgian side Anderlecht 4-3 in a penalty shootout at the end of the UEFA Cup Final, which had finished in a 2-2 aggregate draw after extra-time.

SPURS HISTORY IN TEN GREAT MOMENTS (CONT)

7 – Wembley Wonders

In 1991, a thunderous free-kick from Paul 'Gazza' Gascoigne and two goals from Gary Lineker gave us a 3-1 victory over local rivals Arsenal in the FA Cup semi-final at Wembley. We returned to the 'Home of Football' a month later, beating Nottingham Forest 2-1 after extra-time in the final to win the FA Cup for the eighth time in our history.

8 – A Whole New Ball Game

In 1992, we became founder members of the newly-created FA Premier League. We are one of only six clubs to have competed in every Premier League season since.

9 – Cup Magic

In 2008, we came from a goal behind to beat Chelsea 2-1 in the League Cup Final at Wembley. Striker Dimitar Berbatov scored a second-half penalty to send the match to extra-time and Jonathan Woodgate headed our winner prior to our-then skipper and current Club ambassador Ledley King holding the trophy aloft.

10 – Passport to Europe

In May 2010, a 1-0 win at Manchester City confirmed a top-four finish for Spurs in the Premier League and our first-ever qualification for the UEFA Champions League. We had quite an adventure in Europe's Premier club competition during the 2010/11 season, beating Werder Bremen and FC Twente in the group stage as well as then-European champions Inter Milan. We advanced to the quarter finals by beating AC Milan before being knocked out by Real Madrid.

We returned to the Champions League in 2016/17 by virtue of our third-placed finish in the Premier League the previous campaign. Subsequent top three league finishes mean that 2018/19 is our third consecutive season in the competition of late.

SUPER SPURS QUIZ

1) Who scored our winning goal against Arsenal in February 2018?

2) Which team did we beat 5-4 on the final day of the 2017/18 Premier League season?

3) How many goals did Heung-Min Son score for us during the 2017/18 season?

4) Name the five Spurs players included in England's squad for the 2018 FIFA World Cup?

5) Which nation does Davinson Sánchez represent at international level?

6) From which Football League club did we sign Dele Alli in 2015?

7) What is the name of our Assistant Manager?

8) What year did Spurs become founder members of the Premier League?

9) In which Dutch city did we win the European Cup Winners' Cup in 1963?

10) Who was the manager of our 'Double' winning side in 1961?

11) What is the name of our former goalkeeper who saved two penalties in our 1984 UEFA Cup Final victory over Anderlecht?

12) Who scored our winning goal in our 2008 League Cup Final triumph over Chelsea?

13) Which teams did we face in the International Champions Cup in the summer of 2018?

Answers on page 61

PRE SEASON ROUND-UP

Spurs 6-0 Southend United

Our pre-season preparations got underway with a comfortable victory over League One side Southend in a behind-closed-doors friendly at Hotspur Way. Erik Lamela scored a first-half hat-trick and there were also goals for Fernando Llorente and Lucas Moura as we raced into a 5-0 lead by half-time. Substitute Tashan Oakley-Boothe added our final goal midway through the second period.

Spurs 2-1 Brentford

A late strike from Georges-Kévin Nkoudou saw us come out on top in our clash with Championship team Brentford. Fernando Llorente gave us the lead in the match seven minutes before half-time. Neal Maupay levelled for the Bees in the second-half prior to Nkoudou's winner at Hotspur Way.

Spurs 4-1 Roma

Our American tour began in impressive fashion at the SDCCU Stadium in San Diego, as we came from behind to thrash Italian giants Roma 4-1 in the International Champions Cup (ICC). A first-half brace from Llorente cancelled out Patrik Schick's opener while Lucas also scored twice in the first period.

Spurs 2-2 Barcelona

We overturned a two-goal deficit against La Liga champions Barcelona in our second ICC fixture. Munir and Arthur put Barca two-up by half-time at the historic Rose Bowl Stadium in Los Angeles. Heung-Min Son got a goal back with 16 minutes of the match remaining while Nkoudou equalised a minute later. The Spanish side won 5-3 in the ensuing penalty shootout.

Spurs 1-0 AC Milan

Our American adventure came to an end with a goal from Nkoudou giving us victory over AC Milan at the US Bank Stadium in Minneapolis. Luke Amos, Anthony Georgiou and Kyle Walker-Peters were joined in the starting 11 by fellow academy products TJ Eyoma, George Marsh and Oliver Skipp for their first 'public' starts at first-team level.

Girona 4-1 Spurs

Lucas' fourth goal of pre-season put us one-up in Girona, the Brazilian netting with a fine free-kick. With first-team regulars such as Harry Kane, Hugo Lloris, Dele Alli and Jan Vertonghen still resting after their World Cup exertions, we eventually went down to a 4-1 defeat. The home side's goals came from Juanpe, Anthony Lozano, Portu and Aleix Garcia..

OPPOSITION FILES

These are our Premier League opponents for the current season, which marks our 27th consecutive campaign in the division...

Arsenal
Home Ground: Emirates Stadium (Capacity circa 59,867)

Like ourselves, Arsenal are one of six clubs that have been ever-present in the Premier League since it was established back in 1992. Prior to the start of the 2018-19 season, we had faced our north London rivals 52 times in the division, winning 12 and drawing 21 of those encounters.

AFC Bournemouth
Home Ground: Vitality Stadium (Capacity circa 11,360)

Promoted to the Premier League for the first time back in 2015, AFC Bournemouth are now in their fourth consecutive top-flight season. We won 5-1 on our first league visit to Vitality Stadium back in October 2015, with Harry Kane scoring a hat-trick.

Brighton & Hove Albion
Home Ground: Amex Community Stadium (Capacity circa 30,750)

Last season, the three promoted sides to the Premier League maintained their place in the division for the first time since 2001-02. Brighton & Hove Albion were one of those three teams, with the Seagulls amassing 40 points and finishing 15th in the table. We took four points from a possible six against Albion in 2017-18.

Burnley
Home Ground: Turf Moor (Capacity circa 21,944)

Burnley were one of the Premier League's success stories in 2017-18, with the Clarets finishing seventh in the division and securing a spot in the UEFA Europa League in the process. One of Harry Kane's three hat-tricks for us last season came at Burnley in our 3-0 win in December 2017.

Cardiff City
Home Ground: Cardiff City Stadium (Capacity circa 33,280)

Cardiff City are back in the Premier League for the first time since 2013-14. We beat the Bluebirds in both meetings during their last top flight stay, with Paulinho scoring in our 1-0 win at the Cardiff City Stadium in September 2013 while Roberto Soldado's goal saw us triumph by the same score line in N17 in March 2014.

Chelsea
Home Ground: Stamford Bridge (Capacity circa 41,631)

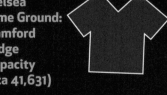

The Blues are another of the Premier League's six ever-present clubs and have won the division five times since 1992. Our 3-1 victory at Stamford Bridge in April 2018 will live long in the memory, while we finished two places higher and seven points better off than our London rivals at the end of the 2017-18 season.

Crystal Palace
Home Ground: Selhurst Park (Capacity circa 25,456)

This season marks Crystal Palace's sixth consecutive campaign in the Premier League – extending their longest-ever stay in the top division. It was on a visit to Selhurst Park that Dele Alli scored the BBC Match of the Day 'Goal of the Season' for the 2014-15 campaign in a 3-1 win over the Eagles in January 2015.

Everton
Home Ground: Goodison Park (Capacity circa 39,572)

The Toffees are currently in their 65th consecutive season in the top flight of English league football – a run bettered only by Arsenal, who are in their 99th. It was against Everton in January 2018 that Harry Kane equalled and then broke Teddy Sheringham's previous record of 97 Premier League goals for us, as we beat the Merseysiders 4-0 at Wembley.

Fulham
Home Ground: Craven Cottage (Capacity circa 25,700)

The west Londoners are back in the Premier League for their first season since 2013-14 and in their 14th campaign in the division overall. Our first Football League meeting with Fulham dates all the way back to 1908 while our first Premier League encounter was a 4-0 victory over the Whites in December 2001.

Huddersfield Town
Home Ground: John Smith's Stadium (Capacity circa 24,500)

We marked our first Premier League visit to Huddersfield Town in impressive fashion in September 2017, with a Harry Kane brace helping us to a 4-0 win. The Terriers finished 16th in the division last season having achieved promotion by beating Reading on penalties in the 2017 EFL Championship Play-Off Final.

Leicester City
Home Ground: King Power Stadium (Capacity circa 32,312)

The Foxes defied the odds back in 2015-16 to win the Premier League title for the first time in the club's history. We have been involved in some memorable matches against Leicester City over the years, not least our 5-4 victory over the East Midlanders on the final day of the 2017-18 season.

Liverpool
Home Ground: Anfield (Capacity circa 54,074)

The Reds are one of English football's most successful clubs, having won 18 top-flight titles and the European Cup/UEFA Champions League on five occasions. A crowd of over 80,000 was at Wembley last season to see our impressive 4-1 win over Liverpool back in October 2017.

Manchester City
Home Ground: Etihad Stadium (Capacity circa 55,097)

City were the run-away winners of the Premier League in 2017-18, amassing 100 points. We have still recorded some memorable results against the Citizens in recent times. Peter Crouch's winner at the Etihad in 2010 saw us qualify for the UEFA Champions League at City's expense, while we did the double over them in 2015-16 with a 4-1 win at the Lane and a 2-1 triumph in Manchester.

Manchester United
Home Ground: Old Trafford (Capacity circa 74,994)

United are the most successful team of the Premier League era having won the division 13 times since 1992 and 20 top-flight titles overall. While we suffered the disappointment of an FA Cup semi-final defeat to the Red Devils in April 2018, we racked up an impressive 2-0 Premier League triumph over them less than three months earlier.

Newcastle United
Home Ground: St James' Park (Capacity circa 52,405)

We were Newcastle United's first-ever Premier League opponents back in August 1993, as we won 1-0 at St James' Park thanks to a goal from Teddy Sheringham. The Magpies returned for their 23rd season in the division in 2017 having won the EFL Championship title and were tenth last season.

Southampton
Home Ground: St Mary's Stadium (Capacity circa 32,505)

The Saints are now in their 20th season in the Premier League, having been one of the division's founder members back in 1992. The Hampshire club achieved their best Premier League finish back in 2015-16, coming sixth while their best overall top-flight finish came in 1983-84 when they were First Division runners-up.

Watford
Home Ground: Vicarage Road (Capacity circa 21,577)

Now in their fourth consecutive season back in the Premier League, after previous stays in 1999-2000 and 2006-07, Watford will be looking to improve on their 14th place finish in 2017-18. The Hornets were our opponents back in March 2007 when our former goalkeeper Paul Robinson scored in a 3-1 win.

West Ham United
Home Ground: London Stadium (Capacity circa 60,000)

West Ham United moved into the London Stadium back in 2016 which had previously hosted the Summer Olympic and Paralympic Games in 2012. We secured our first victory at the venue last season, with a Harry Kane brace and a strike from Christian Eriksen giving us a 3-2 win.

Wolverhampton Wanderers
Home Ground: Molineux (Capacity circa 31,700)

Wolves are competing in the Premier League for the first time since 2011-12, having won the EFL Championship title in impressive fashion in 2018. We beat the Midlanders 3-2 on aggregate in the UEFA Cup Final of 1972, with Martin Chivers scoring twice in our 2-1 triumph at Molineux in the first-leg.

QUIZ AND PUZZLE ANSWERS

P40 Wordsearch

L	Y	L	K	W	L	T	K	L	C	R	X
N	T	H	W	L	P	N	T	W	R	E	T
Q	J	C	O	K	F	G	N	R	K	W	N
L	F	R	K	Z	E	L	X	N	N	O	E
D	I	Q	I	L	N	A	T	J	M	L	H
S	K	M	N	C	N	T	N	J	Z	F	G
D	G	D	G	K	U	C	X	E	H	H	N
L	B	P	Q	B	L	F	M	V	R	C	O
V	H	Z	B	T	N	B	R	R	Y	N	T
X	P	A	L	E	N	A	K	V	T	A	R
B	M	L	G	N	T	M	M	N	Y	L	E
P	E	R	R	Y	M	A	N	Z	F	B	V

P54 Super Spurs Quiz

1) Harry Kane
2) Leicester City
3) 18 goals (in 52 appearances)
4) Dele Alli, Eric Dier, Harry Kane, Danny Rose & Kieran Trippier
5) Colombia
6) MK Dons
7) Jesús Pérez
8) 1992
9) Rotterdam
10) Bill Nicholson
11) Tony Parks
12) Jonathan Woodgate
13) AC Milan, Barcelona & Roma

P41 Numbers Games

Squad Numbers

DELE 20
LLORIS 1
VERTONGHEN 5
KANE 10
ERIKSEN 23

Scoreboards

1901 FA CUP FINAL

SPURS	3
SHEFFIELD UNITED	1

1963 EUROPEAN CUP WINNERS' CUP FINAL

SPURS	5
ATLETICO MADRID	1

1991 FA CUP SEMI-FINAL

SPURS	3
ARSENAL	1

PREMIER LEAGUE – OCT 2017

SPURS	4
LIVERPOOL	1

UEFA CHAMPIONS LEAGUE – NOV 2017

SPURS	3
REAL MADRID	1

WHERE'S CHIRPY?